香港國際詩歌之夜 *2017*
INTERNATIONAL POETRY NIGHTS IN HONG KONG

編輯 Editors

北島 Bei Dao
柯夏智 Lucas Klein
宋子江 Chris Song

老虎的天使

洛爾娜・克羅齊

ANGEL OF TIGERS

LORNA
CROZIER

《老虎的天使》
洛爾娜・克羅齊 著

封面影像：北島

國際統一書號（ISBN）：978-988-237-034-0

出版：中文大學出版社
香港 新界 沙田・香港中文大學
傳真：+852 2603 7355
電郵：cup@cuhk.edu.hk
網址：www.chineseupress.com

Angel of Tigers
By Lorna Crozier

Cover Image: Bei Dao

ISBN: 978-988-237-034-0

Published by The Chinese University Press
The Chinese University of Hong Kong
Sha Tin, N.T., Hong Kong
Fax: +852 2603 7355
E-mail: cup@cuhk.edu.hk
Website: www.chineseupress.com

Printed in Hong Kong

目錄 Contents

洛爾娜・克羅齊
Lorna Crozier

中文翻譯：梁小曼

Fear of Snakes

The snake can separate itself
from its shadow, move on ribbons of light,
taste the air, the morning and the evening,
the darkness at the heart of things. I remember
when my fear of snakes left for good.
It fell behind me like an old skin. In Swift Current
the boys found a huge snake and chased me
down the alleys, Larry Moen carrying it like a green torch,
the others yelling, *Drop it down her back*, my terror
of its sliding in the runnel of my spine (Larry,
the one who touched the inside of my legs on the swing,
an older boy we knew we shouldn't get close to
with our little dresses, our soft skin), my brother
saying, *Let her go*, and I crouched behind the caraganas,
watched Larry nail the snake to a telephone pole.
It twisted on twin points of light, unable to crawl
out of its pain, its mouth opening, the red
tongue tasting its own terror, I loved it then,
that snake. The boys standing there with their stupid hands
dangling from their wrists, the beautiful green
mouth opening, a terrible dark *O*
no one could hear.

懼蛇

蛇能夠脫離自己的
影子，明亮的綢帶繼續爬行
辨別空氣、清晨和黃昏的味道
以及事物幽暗的核心。我想起
當我永遠不再怕蛇。
牠像層老皮在我的身後落下。在斯威夫特卡倫特[1]
男孩們發現一條大蛇，追了我
幾條街，拉里・摩恩提著牠像提著一支綠火炬
其他人在喊，扔到她背上，我驚恐牠
要滑過我的脊柱溝（拉里，那個
秋千上摸我大腿內側的傢伙，
穿小短裙、皮膚柔軟的我們
不可接近的大男孩），我哥哥
說，放過她，我蹲在金雀花後
看著拉里把蛇釘到電線杆上。
牠在發光的兩點間扭動，無法爬行
痛苦撐開了牠的嘴巴，猩紅的
舌頭感受著自身的恐懼，我因此愛牠
這大蛇。男孩們站在那兒，愚蠢的手
垂了下來，那美麗的、綠色的
嘴巴張開，一個幽暗可怕的*O*
沒人聽得見。

1　斯威夫特卡倫特是加拿大的一個地名。

Barren

In the orchard a deer stands on his hind legs.
Out early for a walk, before the village stirs,
she hopes he's come for her, his chest
white with moon-spill, his antlers tall
hard hands, fingers splayed. They touch
the high things humans don't sense are there.
His eyes have dimmed; he's weary
from his travels through the deadfall,
the fallow fields, the raised meadow
of little heartbeats. When he gets close to her,
moving with a shaman's roll from foot to foot,
will he place his mouth upon her mouth
and blow the found one in?

不育

果林裏一隻鹿直直地站著。
村莊蘇醒前的晨間散步
她希望牠為她而來，牠的胸脯
月光下皎潔，牠的鹿角高昂
堅硬的手，張開的手指。牠們觸摸
人感覺不到的高處的事物。
牠的眼神黯淡，為牠的旅途
而疲憊，穿過陷阱
休耕的荒地，高坡的牧場
微小的心跳。牠向她走來
像薩滿祭司邁著顫動交錯的步
牠會用嘴對著她的嘴
將遇見的東西吹進去嗎？

What Comes After

I am my own big dog.
Walk, and I'm at the door,
eat, and I take what I offer,
lie down, and I curl on the floor,
my heavy head between my paws.

I don't need anything but this,
I don't think of what comes after.

I sing the way a dog sings,
I weep the way a dog weeps.
Every night at my feet
I am a big sack of sleep
stinking of me.

以後的事

我是我自己的大狗
走，我就到了門口
吃，給甚麼我吃甚麼
躺下，我蜷伏在地上
沉重的腦袋趴在爪間

除此我沒別的需要
我不去想以後的事

像狗一樣唱歌
像狗一樣嗚咽
每晚趴在我腳邊
我是一個熟睡的口袋
散發著穢氣

More Last Questions

(after W. S. Merwin)

What is the grass?
          The lost ones, talking.

What is the forest?
          Light's tall coffins.

What is the ocean?
          An ancient book of blues
the whales leave behind.

What is the tongue?
          Nobody speaks under the snow.

No, what is the tongue?
          Heel of snake, thumb of earthworm.

No, what is the tongue?

The moon, caught in a trap,
          chews off its right leg
                                        then its left
so it can rise.

更多最後的問題
——仿W. S. 默溫

草是甚麼？
　　迷失的人，在說話

森林是甚麼？
　　光那高聳的棺木

海洋是甚麼？
　　鯨魚留下的
一本遠古的憂鬱之書

舌頭是甚麼？
　　雪中無人言語

不，舌頭是甚麼？
　　蛇的踵，地龍的拇指

不，舌頭是甚麼？

月亮，落入陷阱
　　它咬掉它的右腿
　　　　　　　　　然後是它的左腿
那麼它就能升起

My Mother Lies Dying

Sunshine after
days of rain. A wren
hangs its shadow
on the fence to dry.

What a risk it's taking!
I need a swatch of darkness
to sew a pocket
to hold her final breath.

我的母親臨終

連日雨水後
陽光照耀。一隻鷓鴣
將牠的影子掛在
籬笆上晾乾。

這是多麼冒險！
我需要一塊深色樣布
去縫一個袋子
裹住她最後的呼吸。

From *The Sex Lives of Vegetables*

Lettuce

Raised for one thing
and one thing only,
lettuce is a courtesan
in her salad days.
Under her fancy crinolines
her narrow feet are bound.

選自《蔬菜的性生活》

萵苣

為一個目的而種植
僅僅一個目的，
在她的沙拉生涯裏
萵苣是個交際花。
在她華麗的襯裙下
細窄的腳已被綁

Onions

The onion loves the onion.
It hugs its many layers,
saying *O*, *O*, *O*,
each vowel smaller
than the last.

Some say it has no heart.
It doesn't need one.
It surrounds itself,
feels whole. Primordial.
First among vegetables.

If Eve had bitten it
instead of the apple,
how different Paradise.

洋葱

洋葱熱愛洋葱
它擁抱它層層外衣
念*O*，*O*，*O*
每個元音都小於
上一個

有人說它無心
它並不需要
它與自己為伍
感到完整，原始
蔬菜之初

假如夏娃咬了它
而不是蘋果
天堂將多麼不同

Cabbages

Long-living and slow,
content to dream in the sun,
heads tucked in, cabbages
ignore the caress of the
cabbage butterfly, the soft
sliding belly of the worm.

You know it's crazy
but they lie so still,
so self-contained, you imagine them
laying eggs
in the earth's dark pockets,
expect one morning they'll be gone,
dragging themselves
to the creek behind the house,

making their way
with great deliberation
to the sea.

甘藍

壽而遲緩
喜歡在太陽下做夢
頭埋起，甘藍
對白粉蝶的愛撫
無動於衷，青蟲
那滑動的軟腹

你知道這很奇怪
它們一動不動地躺著
如此克制，你想像
它們產卵在
大地黑色的口袋裏
某天清晨，它們將離開
費力地前往
屋後的小海灣

以巨大的從容
經那裏游向
大海

Potatoes

No one knows
what potatoes do.
Quiet and secretive
they stick together.
So many under one roof
there is talk of incest.

The pale, dumb faces,
the blank expressions.
Potato dumplings.
Potato pancakes.
Potato head.

In dark cellars
they reach across the potato bin
to hold one another
in their thin white arms.

馬鈴薯

沒有人知道
馬鈴薯是做甚麼的
安靜和低調
它們緊緊地挨著
一個屋檐下如此之多
已有亂倫的流言

蒼白，沉默的面孔
茫然的神情
馬鈴薯餃子
馬鈴薯薄餅
馬鈴薯頭

陰暗的地窖裏
穿過馬鈴薯箱子
它們瘦小蒼白的胳膊
相互擁抱

Cucumbers

Cucumbers hide
            in a leafy camouflage,
popping out
when you least expect
like flashers in the park.

The truth is,
they all have an anal
fixation. Watch it
when you bend to pick them.

黃瓜

黃瓜隱藏於
　　繁茂葉子的偽裝裏
在你意想不到時
冒了出來
像公園裏的探射燈

而真相是
它們都有著肛交
迷戀　留意看吧
當你彎腰去摘它們時

Peas

Peas never liked any of it.
They make you suffer for the sweet
burst of green in the mouth. Remember
the hours of shelling on the front steps,
the ping into the basin? Your mother
bribing you with lemonade to keep you there,
popping them open with your thumbs.

Your tongue finds them clitoral
as it slides up the pod.
Peas are not amused.
They have spent all of their lives
keeping their knees together.

豌豆

豌豆從沒喜歡過這事
它們在嘴裏破裂的
甜汁使人受不了，回想起
前門的台階上剝幾小時殼
那落入盆裏的咚咚聲？你的母親
拿檸檬汽水賄賂你，讓你待著
彈開它們，用你的拇指

你的舌頭滑過豆莢時
覺得它們就像陰蒂
豌豆並不愉悅
終其一生它們的
膝蓋都緊緊併攏

Carrots

Carrots are fucking
the earth. A permanent
erection, they push deeper
into the damp and dark.
All summer long
they try so hard to please.
Was it good for you,
was it good?

Perhaps because the earth won't answer
they keep on trying.
While you stroll through the garden
thinking *carrot cake,*
carrots and onions in beef stew,
carrot pudding with caramel sauce,
they are fucking their brains out
in the hottest part of the afternoon.

胡蘿蔔

胡蘿蔔在操
這大地。一個永恆的
勃起，他們往潮濕與
幽暗之地推得更深
整個夏天
他們如此費勁去取悅
你覺得好嗎？
好嗎？

或許是大地不應的緣故
他們推得更深
當你在花園裏散步
想著胡蘿蔔蛋糕
胡蘿蔔洋葱煮牛肉
胡蘿蔔焦糖布丁
他們則在最炎熱的下午
操得靈魂出竅

Ways of Leaving

What I remember best about Rome
is the middle-aged woman
we saw on the path near
the Baths of Caracalla,
sitting in the rain
with her legs straight out,
one elbow leaning on a suitcase,
a plastic kerchief on her head.
A car stopped and a man
leaned out the window, said something
in Italian. She wouldn't look at him,
just shook her head, *no*, *no*, the cars
honking behind him and he pulled away.

She looked solid and respectable,
middle-class. I wondered
what kind of life
she was walking out of,
what was worse than these streets,
this pouring rain.

A block past,
we looked back, saw the car again,
the man rolling down his window,
the woman shouting now, *No!*
We smiled at that,
not knowing then we would leave each other
just as absurdly, three years later,
in a different country,
in the rain.

離開的方式

我對羅馬記憶最深的是
我們在卡拉卡拉浴場
邊上的小路看見的
那個中年女人
她兩腿伸直
坐在雨中
一個胳膊撐在箱子上
戴著塑料頭巾
一輛車停住，一個男人
探出車窗，用意大利語
說了些甚麼。她不看他
只是搖頭，不，不，後面的
車在按喇叭，他開走了。

她看起來可靠，正派
中產階級，我在想
她要出走的
是甚麼樣的生活
有甚麼比這些街道
這場暴雨更糟

走過了一條街
我們往後看，又看見那車
那男人把車窗搖下來
那女人此時咆哮，不！
我們為此笑了
並不知道我們也要分開
三年之後，以同樣的荒誕
在不同的國家
在雨中

That Kind of Heaviness

This morning, a heaviness to everything.
Even the crow is having trouble
lifting the air above its wings. The light
is heavy, the wind in the branches, the
silence between one thought and the next.
It is the feeling that follows
a long afternoon sleep in a strange house,
remember as a child, every object
solid and unfamiliar, holding you there,
alone and not quite human. Watching
the wings of the crow lift and fall,
I think of you, wonder if you sleep
long into the afternoon in another's bed.
I remember your story about the gopher
you shot and shot with a BB gun,
you cold and young, with no regrets.
The gopher pumped so full of pellets
it couldn't run, but dragged its belly
across the grass. That kind of heaviness.
The one the heart knows, its small gut
full of lead.

那種沉重

這個清晨，一切都沉重
連烏鴉要舉起牠翅膀上的
空氣也有困難。光線
很沉，枝條中的風，一個
念頭和另一個念頭間的沉默。
這是在一個陌生的屋子裏
漫長午睡之後的感覺
像孩時的記憶，每個物體
都堅實、陌生，將你固定在那裏
孤獨，不太人性。看著
烏鴉的翅膀飛起飛落
我想著你，想你是否睡了
漫長的午覺，在另一張床。
我想起你囊鼠的故事，
你射擊，用一把彩彈槍射
你冷酷，年輕，沒有悔意
那囊鼠被射得滿是彩彈
牠跑不動，只能拖著肚子
穿過草地。那種沉重。
良心知道的沉重，牠的小心肝
盡是子彈

Without Hands

In memory of Victor Jara, the Chilean musician whose hands were smashed by the military to stop him from playing his guitar and singing for his fellow prisoners in the Santiago stadium. Along with thousands of others, he was tortured and finally killed there in September 1973.

All the machines in the world
stop. The textile machines, the paper machines,
the machines in the mines turning stones to fire.
Without hands to touch them, spoons, forks and knives
forget their names and uses, the baby is not bathed,
bread rises on the stove, overflows the bowl.
Without hands the looms
stop. The music
                                        stops.
The plums turn sweet and sticky and gather flies.

Without hands
                              without those beautiful conjunctions,
those translators of skin, bone, hair,
two eyes go blind
two pale hounds sniffing ahead and doubling back
to tell us
            of hot and cold or the silk of roses after rain
are lost

two terns feeling the air in every feather
are shot down.

Without hands my father doesn't plant potatoes
row on row, build a house for wrens,
or carry me
from the car to bed
when I pretend I'm sleeping.
On wash-days my mother doesn't hang clothes
on the line, she doesn't turn the pages of a book
and read out loud,
or teach me how to lace my shoes.

Without hands my small grandmother
doesn't pluck the chicken for our Sunday meal
or every evening, before she goes to sleep,
brush and brush her long white hair.

沒有手

紀念智利音樂家貝克多・哈拉，政府軍剁掉他的雙手，以阻止他在聖地亞哥體育場為同案犯彈吉他與唱歌。1973年9月，他和另外數千人在飽受酷刑後被殺害。

世上所有的機器都
停頓了。紡織機、造紙機
礦山裏將石頭變成火焰的機器。
沒有手觸摸它們，湯匙和刀叉
遺忘它們的名字和用途，嬰兒無人浴洗，
火爐上的麵包發起，碗在漫溢。
沒有手，那紡車
停頓了。那音樂
　　停頓了。
梅子甜了，變得黏稠，蒼蠅聚集。

沒有手
　　沒有那些美妙的連接詞，
那些皮膚、骨頭和毛髮的譯者；
雙眼要失明
兩條灰白的獵犬在前頭嗅聞又返歸
告知我們
　　涼熱或者雨後綢緞般的薔薇花
不見了

每根羽毛都在感覺著風的兩隻燕鷗
被射落。

沒有手我的父親種植不了一排排的
馬鈴薯，給鷦鷯建築房子，
或者當我假裝
睡著的時候，把我
從車廂抱到床上。
洗濯日裏，我的母親掛不了衣裳
在晾衣繩上，她翻開不了書頁
並高聲朗讀，
或者教我怎麼繫鞋帶。

沒有手我矮小的祖母
拔不了雞毛以備主日的聚餐
或在每個夜晚，入睡之前
一遍又一遍地梳著她長長的白髮

Penis/Bird

There's an Indian story
about a boy who desires a girl
he can't have. She sleeps
in innocence, surrounded
by brothers and sisters,
her parents a hair's breath away.

The boy's penis grows wings,
it flies through the smoke hole
and straight to the girl
as if her lap were full
of breadcrumbs and berries.

I love the story, the penis with wings
more believable than a swan, somehow.
And here, the girl wanted it,
found pleasure
stroking this strange bird
that came from nowhere,
that sang so sweetly
and nested between her thighs,

The breath of her family
close around her,
warming her naked skin.

I like to think of that bird-penis
winging its way back to the body,
a little worse for wear
like a tattered crow
with some feathers missing,
maybe enjoying flight
more than it should,
the boy anxiously
watching the sky.

陰莖 / 鳥

有一個印第安故事
講一個男孩戀慕他
無法擁有的女孩。她入睡
天真無邪，周圍是
兄弟和姐妹
她的父母咫尺之遙

男孩的陰莖長出翅膀
它穿過煙囪
徑直飛向女孩
彷彿她的腿上全是
麵包碎和漿果

我愛這個故事，長翅膀的陰莖
不知何故，它比天鵝更可信
而且，嗨，那女孩喜歡
撫摸著這奇怪的鳥
感到愉悦
它無端而至
歌聲如此甜蜜
盤踞她的大腿之間

家人的呼吸
緊緊地包圍著她
溫暖著她赤裸的肌膚

我老想到那陰莖之鳥
撲閃著翅膀飛回身體
有點兒憔悴
像一隻落魄的烏鴉
丟了一些羽毛
它也許過於享受
那飛行
男孩焦急地
注視著天空

Angel of Tigers

The wheat ripples in the wind
like muscles under the skin
of a great cat.

Never have the fields
been so beautiful, so dangerous.
The beards of wheat flick back and forth,
even when the air is still.

In the long dry heat everything awaits
the gazelle-footed touch of the rain.

老虎的天使

麥浪在風裏
就像一隻大貓的肌肉
毛皮之下起伏。

田野從未
如此美麗，如此危險。
麥穗輕拂搖曳
縱然風是靜止的

漫長的旱熱裏一切在等待
那瞪羚腳步般的雨點

Blizzard

Walking into wind, I lean into my mother's muskrat coat;
around the cuffs her wristbones have worn away the fur.

If we stood still we'd disappear. There's no up or down,
no houses with their windows lit. The only noise is wind

and what's inside us. When we get home my father
will be there or not. No one ever looks for us.

I could lie down and stay right here where snow is all
that happens, and silence isn't loneliness just cold

not talking. My mother tugs at me and won't let go.
Then stops to find her bearings. In our hoods of stars

we don't know if anyone will understand
the tongue we speak, so far we are from home.

暴風雪

走入風中，我依偎在母親的麝鼠皮大衣裏
袖口邊，她的腕骨磨損了皮毛

我們如果站著我們會消失。沒有方向
沒有窗戶亮燈的房子。唯一的噪音是風

和我們身體的聲音。我們到家時父親
也許在那兒，也許不。沒人尋過我們

我可以躺下，留在這個雪就是一切的
地方，沉默不是孤獨，只是寒冷

並不說話。我母親拽著我，不放手。
然後歇息找她的方位。我們繁星的兜帽裏

不知道是否有人能聽懂
我們的語言，在我們離家如此遠的地方

Facts

Did you know an ant has four
olfactory organs on its antennae;
the female mouse, a clitoris? This I learned
from two poets—one famous and American,
the other a student of biology and physics.

Now anything is possible:

Did you know that grass has legs and feet?
That's why it's never still
but runs on the spot like a child in an old gymnasium.

Did you know the moon cleans itself with a tongue
rough as a cat's? It licks and licks until it disappears
then comes up new again, shiny with spittle.

Did you know the yellow butterflies that feed on cabbage
have a temper; the winds, a worrying mother?

Every dusk she stands in the airy doorway of the world
and calls them home.

事實

你知道一隻螞蟻的觸角
有四個嗅覺器官
雌鼠，則有一個陰蒂嗎？這是
兩個詩人告訴我的—— 一個很有名，美國人
另一個是生物和物理系的學生

現在，任何事情都是可能的：

你知道青草長著腿和腳嗎？
所以它從不安靜
像個孩子在舊操場裏原地跑

你知道月亮用和貓舌一般粗糙的
舌頭清潔自身嗎？它舔啊，舔啊，直到消失
然後重新出現，帶著唾沫的光澤

你知道那吃甘藍葉的黃蝴蝶
有脾氣，那風，是一個憂心的母親嗎？

每個傍晚她站在世界那通風的門口
呼喊牠們回家

洛爾娜・克羅齊（加拿大）曾獲加拿大最負盛名的總督文學獎（詩歌）。她也是許多其他獎項的獲得者，包括三次獲得Pat Lowther年度最佳女性詩集獎，最近一次授予2016年的詩集《犯錯的貓》。由於對加拿大文學的貢獻，她還曾經五次被加拿大的大學授予榮譽博士稱號，包括蒙特利爾的麥吉爾大學。她是維多利亞大學名譽退休教授、加拿大皇家學會會員、官佐級加拿大勳章得主，已經出版了十七種詩集。她的詩歌被翻譯成多種語言，其中法語版和西班牙語版數量眾多。她在除了南極洲以外的各大洲都朗讀過詩。

Lorna Crozier (Canada) has received Canada's most prestigious literary award, the Governor General's Award for poetry. She has been the recipient of many others, including three Pat Lowther Awards for the best book of poetry by a Canadian woman, most recently in 2016 for a collection called *The Wrong Cat*. She has also been awarded five honourary doctorates from universities across Canada, including McGill University in Montreal, for her contribution to Canadian literature. A Professor Emeritus at the University of Victoria, a fellow of the Royal Society of Canada, and an Officer of the Order of Canada (the country's highest civilian honour), she has published 17 books of poetry. Her poems have been translated into several languages, including a book-length translation in French and another in Spanish, and she has read in every continent, except Antarctica.

香港國際詩歌之夜 2017
International Poetry Nights in Hong Kong 2017

主辦單位 Organizers

香港中文大學文學院
Faculty of Arts, The Chinese University of Hong Kong
香港詩歌節基金會有限公司
Hong Kong Poetry Festival Foundation Limited

協辦單位 Co-organizers

香港中文大學中國文化研究所
Institute of Chinese Studies, The Chinese University of Hong Kong
香港中文大學出版社
The Chinese University Press
香港大學美術博物館
The University Museum and Art Gallery, The University of Hong Kong
香港大學文學院
Faculty of Arts, The University of Hong Kong
香港科技大學賽馬會高等研究院
Jockey Club Institute for Advanced Study, Hong Kong University of Science and Technology
香港科技大學人文學部
Division of Humanities, Hong Kong University of Science and Technology
廣州時刻文化傳播有限公司
Moment Communications
活字文化
MoveableType Legacy (Beijing) Co., Ltd.
當當
DANGDANG

贊助 Sponsors

中國會 The China Club
北京匡時國際拍賣有限公司 Beijing Council International Auction Co., Ltd.
先鋒公益基金會 UCF Charity Foundation Limited
卓爾書店 the zall bookstore
斑馬谷文化發展有限公司 Zebra Valley Culture Development
馮鑫牟希文夫婦 Feng Xin (Larry) and Mu Xi Wen (Maggie)
蓮華書院 Lianhua Academy